Twenty Inspirations of God

by

Jerry Barfield

www.rdtalleybooks.com

Plainsboro, New Jersey

The Holy Bible version referenced in this book is the King James Version.

The dictionary referenced in this book is The Funk & Wagnalls Standard Family Dictionary, Volumes 1 and 2, Copyright © 1947, 1950, 1953, 1956, and 1961 by Funk & Wagnalls Company.

Cover Designed by Michela Fellows

ISBN: 978-1-7342540-5-1

R.D. Talley Books Publishing
P.O. Box 45
Plainsboro, New Jersey 08536
www.rdtalleybooks.com

To God, for without His Holy Spirit I would've never written this.

To *my* brothers and sisters in Christ who have encouraged me to write this book.

Table of Contents

Introduction

When much is given, much is required! Greetings in the name of Christ Jesus, as these words echo loud and clear in my spirit. It seems that the Lord has given me a gift and this gift is what I want to share with you.

As you read this book that God has given me, I pray that the Holy Spirit will give you a spirit of understanding of these words I've written for you. For it's only God's glory that I've desired to share with you.

May Christ Jesus bless and keep you one and all and may these inspirations be a revelation to your edification!

God bless you!

Come Now and Let Us Reason Together

(Isaiah 1:18)

It says in God's Word, in the Book of Isaiah, to "Let us reason," because if we're able to comprehend, we will be able to reason. "Come now, and let us reason." Reasoning is a way that man (and woman and children) can solve the everyday problems that Satan throws in our pathway.

Reason is defined as (1) "a motive or a cause for an action, belief, thought," meaning that the motive of those who serve Christ is to glorify Him so that he may be lifted up; (2) "an explanation for or defense of an action, belief, justification, etc.," meaning that when we praise Him for what He does in our lives, man can see God for who He is: a way-maker, problem solver, redeemer, wonderful counselor, bright, morning star, comforter, dayspring, etc.; (3) "the faculty of thinking logically," meaning that when we keep our hearts and our minds on God, we will be able to see clearer and be able to look into His Word even deeper and think on His Word being presented to us even better.

8

Another definition is (4) "good judgment; common sense," meaning that the only good judgment in our Christian walk comes from no one but Christ and to the Christian, that's common sense. The last definition is (5) "a normal state of mind; sanity," meaning that doing God's will, God's way and letting God be set in our minds and hearts is a normal state of mind. But since we're a "peculiar people", the world believes that we've lost our sanity. But by keeping, staying, praying, and obeying God, we may obtain more knowledge than a college professor.

And it takes nothing more or nothing less than the will of the Lord to guide you, keep you, restore you, revive you, and protect you. In closing, if you ask God for any or all of these things, I know, beyond the shadow of a doubt, He will deliver them unto you. Let God have the praise, honor, and glory in your life and He will change your life. So, rejoice in His holy name!

Be Quiet and Listen

(Mark 4:9)

As Jesus spoke the parable of the sower, they sat, mouths closed, and listened. They listened to the One whom they knew could lead not only them, but others to the path; the path of salvation. Salvation, above all the other things in life, is the main thing that men and women, whether they be saved or unsaved, clothed or naked, crazy or right-minded, rich or poor, weak or strong, are all craving. We all strive for some type of salvation.

Now, I don't know about you, but the Bible tells me that you just can't buy, rent, borrow, steal, or lend out salvation, because of where it comes from. Plus, it's not given out haphazardly, like candy, which you can just give to whoever you want. Salvation is a gift, the most perfect and righteous gift from God, because the blood of Jesus Christ, who died on Calvary's cross, was the price of salvation. So, if you just be quiet and listen, you'll hear God because it's that small still (and occasionally loud) voice that He has to give us our commands, to be what He wants us to be, to do what He wants us to do and to say what He wants us to say so that He, being above all things, obtains what's rightfully his: Glory!

In the military, commands come in two parts: preparatory command and follow-through command, or what you carry out. Your preparatory command prepares you to do something, i.e., "About face!" The first part tells you which way to go or to get ready to complete the command. The secondary, or follow-through command is the actual command that tells you what to do, where to go, or how to do it. Jesus didn't have to tell the disciples to be quiet and listen because His words were enough. He was able to captivate a crowd to let it be known that "He that hath ears to hear, let him hear," but first we are to be quiet and listen!

Because that's the way the world is today, you have so many things that Satan tries to put up and put in the way of God's voice that he doesn't want you to listen to. Satan knows that if you do just be quiet and listen to God's voice, he will be fighting a battle he knows is lost.

So when you're in your car, house, secret closet, job, church, no matter where, when you hear God's voice, the only thing that you should do is be quiet and listen!

Wait On the Lord

(Psalms 27:14)

When David, being full of faith, had felt his faith start to wane, he knew that only God could deliver him from anything and everything, no matter how big, no matter how small. Being human, David saw his enemies gather against him, but he feared not and was patient with God.

A lot of times in our lives we have things happen, but when they do, it's not when we want them to happen. So, we try to put God on a timetable to determine when we want things in our lives. But we should (although sometimes we don't) remember that our time is not God's time and God's time is not our time. So, what must we do then? Wait! Wait on the Lord. It says in James 1:17 that "Every good gift and every perfect gift is from above, and cometh down from the Father of Lights, with whom is no variableness, neither shadow of turning."

The Lord says in Psalms 27:14 to "Be of good courage, and he shall strengthen thine heart; Wait, I say, on the Lord," meaning fear nothing from Satan

13

because he has no power. All he has is deception. If you allow yourself to be deceived by him, then, and only then, will you believe that he has power. Use the "good courage" that Jesus has given you, which is from (1) His fellowship (2) His word (3) His blood that he spilled on Calvary's cross. Through these things, Jesus gives us courage and strengthens our hearts to contain more of Him and to be like Him, so we may take away all of Satan's deception.

Continue to fellowship with the Lord in prayer, fellowship with other saints, stay constantly in His Word, and give thanks and praises to Him because God, and not anything we do, deserves the real credit for anything we do in life! And only in doing those things will you have that "good courage" to combat Satan because God will "strengthen thine heart" to go against the trials and tribulations that we go through in our lives. If we are to do anything in God's richness and glory, all we have to do is "Wait, I say, on the Lord."

The Doorway To Salvation

(John 10:9)

As Jesus spoke the parable of the door, the Pharisees had no understanding of what was being told when he said in verse 7, "Verily, verily, I say unto you, I am the door of the sheep." However, as caretakers, shepherds are to make sure that the sheep that are under their charge are taken care of and have safe passage.

In many places in the Bible, Jesus describes Himself as many things. For example, in John 6:51, He refers to Himself as bread. He says, "I'm the living bread which came down from Heaven: If any man eat of this bread, he shall live for ever: and the bread that I will give is my flesh which I will give for the life of the world." He also said in John 8:12, "I am the light of the world: He that followeth me shall not walk in darkness, but shall have the light of life." But, at this time in 10:7, he says, "I'm the door of my sheep."

He also said, "All that ever came before me are thieves and robbers." A thief and a robber will try to steal and kill because all he's trying to do is take what belongs to you and make it his. They that are in the world will try and find a way or steal a way to: (1) have salvation; (2) get eternal life; (3) get into Heaven through any human means possible. But we who are in the Word know and feel better, not desperate about it all because we know the true way.

Now, we all know what John 3:16 says and what Romans 10:9 says, but this is what John 10:9 says: "I'm the door: by me if any man enter in, he shall be saved, and shall go in and out, and find pasture." Jesus shall: (1) heal us; (2) deliver us; (3) feed us; (4) keep us safe. All we have to do is walk on through the door, and we shall be saved. As long as He is the shepherd and we're the sheep who hears His voice, then and only then will we be able to walk right on through, to the doorway to salvation!

The Chosen Ones Of God

(John 15:16 and 19)

When Jesus spoke to the disciples in these verses, he had explained to them already about him being "the true vine," and them being able to "abide in me," telling them that "ye are the branches," having said in John 15:10 "If ye keep my commandments, ye shall abide in my love; even as I have kept my Father's commandments, and abide in his love."

In the beginning, we, being Gentiles, were not the real chosen ones of God, but rather it was the Jews. They however, being rebellious, refused this grace which was shared amongst the Gentiles, who were given the option of becoming Christians, which we are, since we've confessed Christ as our Lord and Savior, been washed in his blood, and believe in Him and His Word.

Chosen, as defined in the Funk & Wagner Dictionary, is an adjective as: (1) made an object of choice, selected (isn't it wonderful to know that you've been "made an object of choice" by God?); (2) elect.

Now the latter should make you feel even more special because God elected you to be with him. Isn't that great?

John 15:16 says, "Ye have not chosen me, but I have chosen you, and ordained you, that ye should go and bring forth fruit, and that your fruit should remain: that whatsoever ye shall ask of the Father in my name, he may give it you."

Now, it wasn't our choice to choose God. It was his and his alone because a lot of times if it were our choice, we probably would've never made it. "And ordained you." Now the dictionary defines the word ordain as a transitive verb, which is a verb that requires a complement to complete its meaning. Ordain is: (1) to order or decree; enact, meaning that we are ordered to "bring forth fruit" that's acceptable to God; (2) to predestine; destine: said of God, fate, etc.

It's amazing that God, being so full of wisdom and knowledge, had already made this choice in our lives.

Now if we would've made the decision, we never would've gone God's way and his decision is good enough. Ordain also means: (3) to invest with ministerial or priestly functions.

In one way or another, we all are involved in a ministry, which is to teach, reach, and preach to a dying world the Gospel.

"That ye should go and bring forth fruit and that fruit should remain," and the fruit that we're to get are souls to live a life for Jesus. And in doing so, there's a promise "that whatsoever ye shall ask of the Father in my name, he may give it you," saying that as long as God gets the glory, then the promise is kept.

But remember, there's also a warning in verse 19, which says: "If ye were of the world, the world would love his own: but because ye are not of the world, but I have chosen you out of the world, therefore the world hateth you." Satan will try to' do whatever he can to stop us from saving souls for Jesus Christ. Now aren't you glad that you're one of the chosen ones of God?

Resurrect Your Life

(John 11:25 and 26)

Jesus describes Himself not just as one, but two things in this piece of Scripture when He came, after four days' delay, to see his friend Lazarus. Mary and Martha had been just waiting for Jesus to come and to help their brother.

Now, a lot of times all we do is wait for Jesus to come and help us out and that's the end, like it's only in our darkest days that we call Him to save us like Superman coming to the rescue. But this isn't the way God works because if we did that, we wouldn't have any need for him in our better days.

Yes, God provides for us and feeds us and watches over us and strengthens us, but He doesn't just do it in our bad times. He does it in our good times as well. Because we do die daily, we need to be resurrected. Resurrect is a transitive verb meaning: (1) to bring back to life, raise from the dead (and because we were in the world, dead in sin, it was only by the blood of Jesus and confession of Him as Lord and Savior that we're "back to life," living a life for

Jesus); (2) to bring back into use or to notice, saying that now that we're "back into use," to serve the Lord so that he may be glorified.

Our third use is to raise from the physical death. Jesus knew what he went to Bethany for, when the disciples didn't: to bring new life back to Lazarus. Martha and Mary heard that Jesus arrived, but only Martha came to speak to Him, saying: "Lord, if thou hadst been here, my brother had not died."

Martha also knew what Jesus could do because she knew that He was the Son of God, and said: "But I know, that even now, whatsoever thou wilt ask of God, God will give it thee." Jesus reassured her that Lazarus would rise again. John 11:25 and 26 continues, saying: "Jesus said unto her, 'I am the resurrection, and the life: he that believeth in me, though he were dead, yet shall he live: and whosoever liveth and believeth in me shall never die. Believest thou this?" As long as we keep our eyes, mind, heart stayed on God and believe on and in Him, we will have life eternal. Just stay focused on Him and He will resurrect your life.

Silver and Gold

(Proverbs 16:16)

Throughout time there always has been some kind of object to determine wealth, and for a long time, it's been silver and gold. Now if you look at your chemical tables, you will see that their atomic numbers are nowhere close, but they have one number in common, which is 7. This remind me of Matthew 18:21 and 22: "Then came Peter to him and said, Lord, how oft shall my brother sin against me, and I forgive him? Jesus saith unto him, 'I say not unto thee, until seven times. But, until seventy times seven."

Now, silver is also known as argentum. Its chemical symbol is AG and atomic number is 47, which means that there are 47 protons (or positive charges) in the atomic nucleus. Gold is known as aurum. It has the symbol AU and an atomic number of 79. Now with all of this, these are considered "precious metals," but in the Word, there are many references to these "precious metals" and we'll touch on that shortly. First, we're going to take you to where you can "mine" this "precious metal" called silver.

First, we go to 1 Kings 10:27 in which it's described as "silver to be in Jerusalem as stones". Then we step on over to Job in 22:25. "Yea, the Almighty shall be thy defense, and thou shalt have plenty of silver." And in 27:16 and 17, "Though he heap up silver as the dust, and prepare raiment as the clay; he may prepare it, but the just shall put it on, and the innocent shall divide the silver." Now, we go to Psalms 12:6 where "The words of the Lord are pure words: as silver tried in a furnace of earth purified seven times." In Psalms 66:10 it says, "For thou, O God, hast proved us, thou has tried us, as silver is tried."

Now we head into Ecclesiastes 5:10 in which the love of the "precious metal" is stated, "He that loveth silver shall not be satisfied with silver, nor he that loveth abundance with increase: this is also vanity." In Isaiah 1:22 it says, "Thy silver is become dross". In Jeremiah 6:30 it regards the wicked. "Reprobate silver shall men call them, because the Lord hath rejected them."

In Amos 8:6, in which exploiters are able to purchase men, says "that we may buy the poor for silver," and in Matthew 26:15 and 16, Judas Iscariot agrees to betray Jesus "for 30 pieces of silver. And from that time he sought opportunity to betray him." As we see in all these scriptures, silver is used: (1) "as stones" to (2) "have plenty" (3) "heap up," etc. (4) "divide" (5) "be tried" (6) "been purified", but also we're not to (1) "loveth it" (2) let it "become dross" (3) "buy the poor" and we should "reprobate" it. If we abide by these teachings, then we can do our master's will.

Hang on! Now we're "going for the gold" so to speak. Now come with me and we will find gold. Even though it's everywhere when we look in God's Word, we find where "The gold of that land is good." In Job 31:24, he protests "If I have made gold my hope, or have said to the fine gold, thou art my confidence..."

Looking back in Proverbs 8:10, we are to receive "knowledge rather than choice gold." And in Proverbs 17:3 it states, "And the furnace for gold: but the Lord trieth the hearts." In Psalms 19:10, David sings out on the judgments of God, saying, "More to be desired are they than gold, than much fine gold." Having both metals according to the world is good, but this is what God's Word says about both silver and gold. First, we go to Deuteronomy 17:17, which says, "Neither shall multiply wives to himself, that his heart turn not away: neither shall he greatly multiply to himself silver and gold." And from there to Job 3:15, he speaks of "princes that had gold, who filled their house with silver."

Also in Job 28:1 that "Surely there is a vein for silver and a place for gold where they find it." But hear God speaking through Haggai in 2:8: "The silver is mine, and the gold is mine, saith the Lord of host." Now we take our "golden trip" into the New Testament where we travel to Acts 3:6. "Then Peter said, 'silver and gold have I none;". We go into James' Epistle in which he warned the rich men of God's judgment in James 5:3, saying, "Your gold and silver is cankered; and the rest of them shall be a witness against you, and shall eat your flesh as it were fire."

In closing, as wise as God made Solomon, he spoke in Proverbs 16:16, "How much better is it to get wisdom than gold!

And to get understanding rather to be chosen than silver!" By dwelling in his word, we can get this because we know that God's Word is better than silver and gold.

What Is Faith?

(Hebrews 11:1, 5 and 6)

We have been told to have faith in something in our everyday lives because if we don't have faith, we have nothing. Now, in our everyday lives, there lies faith, whether if it be in God, our other halves, mates, parents, brothers, sisters, etc. But what is faith? Let's look at two different sources.

First, according to man's definition, it's a noun and it is confidence in or dependence on a person, statement or thing as trustworthy. You see, when we first came into this world, we had a dependence on our parents because no matter what happened, we knew that they wouldn't let anything happen to us if they could help it.

According to man, faith is also belief without need of a certain proof. In these days that we are living in, man thinks that we know that we have faith in God. Why? Because we still live and breathe.

But what does this have to do with this meaning? Because we can do these things, we don't have a "need of certain proof," knowing that God works in our lives.

According to man, faith is also belief in God or in the Scripture or other religious writings. We, being children in Christ, believe and live in and of Him. We believe in Him because of our confession of who Jesus is, and of Him, because of what He has (a) brought us from (b) brought us in (c) brought us through (d) will bring us to.

Additionally, according to man, faith is a system of religious belief. Now this is tough. Well, our "system" is (a) reading God's Word (b) seeking His face (c) living a life that is acceptable in the eyes of God so that when we live out our lives, our families, friends, and others can see Jesus in us and through us, therefore the world can know that He still lives.

Next, according to man, faith is anything given adherence or credence. Since we know that God's word has no lie in it, we not only give adherence, in other words, follow what it says, but also because we do know that these things have happened.

The words have that much more "credence." Lastly faith is allegiance. Since we take up the side of God in our lives, that is our "allegiance" to Him.

Now that we have gone through man's definitions, we now go to the Father's definitions. Paul starts off in Hebrews 11:1 by saying what it actually is: "Now faith is the substance of things hoped for, the evidence of things not seen." Now, we don't need to see it (although some do), but if we stay focused on Jesus and keep applying his principles to our daily lives, our faith will continue to grow and become more evident.

Hebrews 11:5 and 6 reads "By faith Enoch was translated that he should not see death; and was not found, because God had translated him: For before his translation he had this testimony, that he pleased God. But without faith it is impossible to please him: For he that cometh to God must believe that he is, and that he is a rewarder of them that diligently seek him." And there are so many others that you can find.

So, as long as you (1) read (2) pray, and (3) stay, then you won't have to ask, "What is faith?" Because if you live in and rely on Jesus, you will know and have faith!

Be Humble

(1 Peter 5:6)

It seems that the easiest things in life are more often the hardest to obtain, but there's no unexplained reason as to why. Take, for example, accepting salvation. Now it didn't cost us anything in a physical, emotional, or even in a financial sense, so why does it seem so hard? The same is so about being humble. Now a lot of people have a very bad perception about being humble. People in the world feel that in being humble, they are soft or weak, when in fact they're the strongest people you can ever meet. And if you give me just a few minutes of your time, I'll let the Holy Spirit explain it to you through this.

Now humble, defined as an adjective, means: (1) free from pride or vanity; modest, because we know that the Holy Spirit will not remain vibrant in an unclean temple (body), and if we have pride, then it's unclean. Why? We are trying to make ourselves something we are not. (2) Lowly in station, condition, etc; unpretentious.

So why should we pretend we are something we are not, thinking we are this and that when we are nothing at all without Christ.

There are multiple other definitions, but guess what? Good things happen to people who are humble. Not only good, but great things that couldn't have been seen before as in 2 Chronicles 34:27: "Because thine heart was tender, and thou didst humble thyself before God, when thou heardest his words against this place, and against the inhabitants thereof, and humbledst thyself before me, and didst rend thy clothes, and weep before me; I have even heard thee also, saith the Lord."

David himself had said in Psalms 10:17, "Lord, thou hast heard the desire of the humble: Thou wilt prepare their heart, thou wilt cause thine ear to hear:" But a good illustration of being humble comes from Proverbs 16:19 in which Solomon says, "Better it is to be of an humble spirit with the lowly, than to divide the spoil with the proud."

A great reward of being humble is found in Isaiah 57:15, saying, "For thus saith the high and lofty one that inhabiteth eternity, whose name is holy; I dwell in the high and holy place, with him also that is of a contrite and humble spirit, to revive the spirit of the humble, and to revive the heart of the contrite ones."

Jesus Himself teaches us to be humble as is said in Matthew 18:4, "Whosoever therefore shall humble himself as this little child, the same is greatest in the Kingdom of Heaven." And in Matthew 23:12 as well: "And whosoever therefore shall exalt himself shall be abased; and he that shall humble himself shall be exalted." Now, I don't know about you, but this is what I feel we should strive for. With blessings like this, would it be silly not to be anything else but humble?

But the biggest and the best is yet to arrive if we look to where James speaks in 4:6, "But he giveth more grace. Wherefore he saith God resisteth the proud, but giveth grace unto the humble." And in closing, in James 4:10, "Humble yourselves in the sight of the Lord, and he shall lift you up," and also 1 Peter 5:5. "Likewise, ye younger, submit yourselves unto the elders.

Yea, all of you be subject one to another, and be clothed with humility: for God resisteth the proud, and giveth grace to the humble."

So, we should do as in 1 Peter 5:6: "Humble yourselves therefore under the mighty hand of God, that he may exalt you in due time." Now tell me, isn't this the way we should be? Because one of primary things He wants us to be is humble!

Redeemed

(Psalms 107:2)

Every now and then, Satan tries to steal the joy that the Lord has put into our hearts and souls. Why? Because we, being the children of the light, have been redeemed in the eyes of God. And because of that, Satan puts stumbling blocks in our pathways, throws fiery darts to prick us, and sends his demons to cause chaos in our lives. But no matter what, if we remain steadfast in our minds, hearts, bodies, and souls in Jesus, we are redeemed!

Now, the word redeem is a very special word with a very special meaning: a transitive verb meaning "to regain possession of by paying a price", and the price that was paid is the shedding of the blood of Jesus on Calvary's Cross, which we all know is the greatest price of all.

In 2 Samuel 4:9, as Rechab and Baanah slew Ishbosheth and brought back his head for David to see: "

And David answered Rechab and Baanah his brother, the sons of Rimmon the Beerothite, and said unto them, 'As the Lord liveth, who hath redeemed my soul out of all adversity."

Isaiah had written many things about being redeemed, beginning in Isaiah 1:27 when he had spoken to this wonderful city, "Zion shall be redeemed with judgment, and her converts with righteousness." In Isaiah 35:9 as he spoke of where we, as the Saints of God will be, that "No lion shall be there, nor any ravenous beast shall go up there on, it shall not be found there; but the redeemed shall walk there."

In Isaiah 43:1, the Lord comforts us with his promises, saying, "But now thus saith the Lord that created thee, O Jacob, and he that formed thee O Israel, fear not: for I have redeemed thee, I have called thee by thy name. Thou art mine." I know that I myself am truly blessed when God says that He stated that I'm his. It seems it does not get any better.

But it does, as He says in Isaiah 44:22: "I have blotted out, as a thick cloud, thy transgressions, and, and as a cloud, thy sins: return unto me; for I have redeemed thee."

This is what God wants us to do, to go back to Him and we should do so with much joy and gladness!

There's more in Isaiah 51:11 in which He says, "Therefore the redeemed of the Lord shall return and come with singing unto Zion; and everlasting joy shall be upon their head: they shall obtain gladness and joy; and sorrow and mourning shall flee away." And in Isaiah 52:3: "For thus saith the Lord, ye have sold yourselves for nought; and ye shall be redeemed without money."

Zacharias' prophecy is recorded in Luke 1:68: "Blessed be the Lord God of Israel; for he hath visited and redeemed his people." And as we look into 1 Peter 1:18 and 19, it states how we were redeemed: "Forasmuch as *ye* know that ye were not redeemed with corruptible things, as silver and gold, from your vain conversation received by tradition from your fathers; but with the precious blood of Christ, as of a lamb without blemish and without spot."

In Revelation 5:9, John writes of when the lamb, being Christ Jesus, comes forward to open the book with the seven seals: "And they sung a new song, saying, Thou art worthy to take the book, and to open the seals thereof: for thou wast slain, and hast redeemed us to God by thy blood out of every kindred, and tongue, and people, and nation;"

And finally, as David has written in Psalms 107:2, foreshadowing those who acknowledge Christ Jesus, "Let the redeemed of the Lord say so, whom he hath redeemed from the hand of the enemy." So remember, no matter how much Satan tries to attack and block off your blessings and anything else, all you have to do is give it all to Jesus and you will be and feel redeemed!

Ten Things to Remember

1. As Christians, we are to come now and let us reason together!
2. To hear from God, we have to be quiet and listen!
3. To know how He works, we have to wait on the Lord!
4. When we have accepted Him, we can walk through the doorway of salvation!
5. We are blessed because we are the chosen ones of God!
6. Because you took Jesus, He was able to resurrect your life!
7. When you have Jesus, you don't need silver and gold!
8. To totally trust in God, you have to know what is faith.
9. To be like Christ, we have to learn to be humble!
10. Stay with God, because of Him you were redeemed!

Selah!

Upon This Rock

(Matthew 16:18)

"And I say also unto thee, that thou art Peter, and upon this rock I will build my church; and the gates of Hell shall not prevail against it." Those are some of the words Jesus said to Peter after asking the disciples in accordance with Matthew 16:15, "But whom say ye that I am?" In verse 16 Peter's reply, since he knew whom he was speaking to, was this: "Thou art the Christ, the Son of the Living God."

Now, when we hear these words "upon this rock," we know what this "rock" means, but it has a lot of meanings, as for instance in the songs that go "Jesus is the rock in a weary land" or "Jesus is the rock of my salvation." When we want a strong foundation, we want it on something solid, something strong, something that can't and won't move in the slightest breeze.

Something that won't make you sink and something that will and shall endure the test of time. Those of us who run this Christian race know that rock, that strong and mighty rock, is the Word of God.

And as long as we can build on God's Word, we have a strong and solid foundation that time, trials, tribulations, and Satan cannot harm or destroy.

Now sometimes, we can build things on what may look solid, but can move the second you say "Boo!" But with this rock for an anchor, we will stay firm and we will stand! And what did Jesus say He would build on this rock? "My church." Now, we know that a church is God's house and people, and if using the Word to build God's house is good enough for Him, shouldn't we be able to build our home with it? Because we should have our home life like our church life, which is strong in Christ, we should take time in praising, glorifying, and lifting up the name of Jesus in our home as well as church so that our homes should be like our second church. This ensures that God can obtain the glory that He deserves.

"And the gates of Hell shall not prevail against it." Because you're living a life for Jesus, Satan is going to try to see if he can set up his household there, which is why he tries to put up his gates, so he can try to lock us up in Hell, that is, if we let him.

But if the foundation of our life, church and home is built upon the Word of God, then you know that "the gates of Hell shall not prevail against it." But should Hell's gates raise up, use the Word of God to knock them back down and let Satan know what your true foundation is, and that it's "upon this rock!"

Watch Your Step

(Psalms 37:23)

When you accept Christ in your life and allow him to take control of it, it changes your life because your character and perspective in life change as well. But some of the people who knew you before you accepted the Lord are always going to watch you to criticize you any way they can, so they will watch your steps.

Job, who had much favor in God's eyes for He had blessed Job, because he was able to watch his steps even in the worst of times, let the people know his faith, saying in Job 31:7, "If my step hath turned out of the way, and mine heart walked after mine eyes, and if any blot hath cleaved to mine hands."

But earlier he had to proclaim his integrity; he said in Job 23:11, "My foot hath held his steps, his ways have I kept, and not declined." Also, as we turn to Proverbs 4:12, in which Solomon shows the instruction from his parents, it says "When thou goest, thy steps shall not be straightened; and when thou runnest, thou shalt not stumble."

And also in Proverbs 16:9, Solomon allows us to know "a man's heart deviseth his way: but the Lord directeth his steps."

David, another man who found favor in the eyes of God, has shown us in Psalms 37:31 regarding a righteous one that "The law of his God is in his heart; none of his steps shall slide." In Psalms 85:13 it explains to us that as we walk in God "righteousness shall go before him; and shall set us in the way of his steps." In Psalms 119:113, at all times, we should ask God to "order my steps in thy word: and let not any iniquity have dominion over me."

Jeremiah 10:23 says, "O Lord, I know that the way of man is not in himself: it is not in man that walketh to direct his steps." He tells us who directs our steps and is underscored in Psalms 37:23, which says that, "The steps of a good man are ordered by the Lord: and he delighteth in his way." So, remember brethren, watch your step!

Wisdom and Understanding

(Job 28:28)

The thing about wisdom is that it's given in time as effort is applied, the same as understanding. You can have knowledge, but if you don't have any understanding, you are lost, because what good is wisdom if you don't have understanding?

Now both wisdom and understanding, in some degree, are intertwined with each other, because you need understanding to know wisdom and wisdom to get the understanding. Let's look at five points of wisdom and understanding.

First is the wisdom of Christ as told in Isaiah 11:2, as he spoke about Jesse when he said, "And the Spirit of the Lord shall rest upon him, the spirit of wisdom and understanding, the spirit of counsel and might, the spirit of knowledge; and of the fear of the Lord."

Second, we have the promised wisdom in Daniel as he told Anoch, the king's captain, that he would reveal to the king the interpretation of his dream and the secret was revealed in Daniel 2:20 and

21 when "Daniel answered and said, 'blessed be the name of God for ever and ever: for wisdom and might are his: and he changeth the times and the seasons: he removeth kings, and setteth up kings: he giveth wisdom unto the wise, and knowledge to them that know understanding:' "

Third, comes the preciousness of wisdom described by Solomon with much joy in Proverbs 3:13: "Happy is the man that findeth wisdom, and the man that getteth understanding."

Fourth, Solomon tells us first and foremost what we must do in Proverbs 4:7: "Wisdom is the principal thing; therefore get wisdom: and with all thy getting get understanding."

But most of all, if there was a man (other than Jesus), any man who would know anything about wisdom and understanding, it would be one who found favor in the eyes of God, Job. And all the things he had said and that happened to him, he fully wrapped up very neatly and put a bow on it when he said in Job 28:28, "And unto man he said, 'Behold, the fear of the Lord, that is wisdom; and to depart from evil is understanding'."

So, my brethren, remember that in order to have true wisdom, you need true understanding and true understanding is true wisdom!

Are You Pressed?

(Philippians 3:14)

"I press toward the mark for the prize of the high calling of God in Christ Jesus." Paul writes this to the saints at Philippi during a time of imprisonment to remind them what to strive for, reach, and obtain. It's in our everyday life where we are always pressed to do things. In the morning we are pressed to awaken (unless God calls us up during the evening), pressed to prepare ourselves for another day. We are pressed to accomplish either work or our other daily activities, and then we are pressed to ensure that all is well after the day is over.

As we go through the day, we should remember that this Christian race that we run is a very long and tiring race, for as it's said in Ecclesiastes 9:11: "I returned, and saw under the sun, that the race is not to the swift, nor the battle to the strong, neither yet bread to the wise, nor yet riches to men of understanding, nor yet favor to men of skill; but time and chance happeneth to them all."

Mind you, this isn't a one hundred-yard dash we are talking about here. This is a marathon and it's not until Christ returns or when He calls us up that this race is over for us all.

Are you pressed by the trials and the tribulations of this world? By the fiery darts that are thrown at you? By the demons that Satan sends against you? Have no fear. Just remember what Paul said in Ephesians 6:10: "Finally, my brethren, be strong in the Lord, and in the power of his might."

As we are being pressed, remember that we are being pressed because we are reaching and striving for a goal that can be obtained. Satan tries to make it harder than it really is. Because you are pressing "toward the mark for the prize of the high calling of God in Christ Jesus", Satan is going to press you, but if Jesus lives in you, you can press right back because when Christ rose from the grave according to Matthew 28:18, "And Jesus came and spake unto them, saying, 'All power is given unto me in Heaven and in earth.'" So if he has, (and does have) "all power," just how much do you think Satan have?

But remember, as you go about doing God's work and God's will, you will be pressed. However, as you talk to God and leave your burdens with him, the load will be lighter. Although we are either going through, coming out of or going into a storm, remember that this too shall pass, and we will be stronger than ever. So tell me, as you work for the Lord, are you pressed?

Be Still

(Psalms 46:10)

We are always rushing to do this and that, going here and there, etc., but we don't take time to relax. You can't hear what God is saying if you don't take time to be still. We have to take time to be still in Him, so that way He can do His work in us for His glory. This is essential because we are here to show a sin-sick world, whose people are running at neck-break speed, going to a place that wasn't made nor prepared for us.

To be still is to be patient, watching and waiting for instructions from a king who has seen many battles and never lost. As an army soldier, in order to get the correct order or command, you have to be still, or you will be doing one thing while the rest will be doing the true assignment. As the Lord said, when he came to Jeremiah in the destruction of the Philistine, in Jeremiah 47:6, "O thou sword of the Lord, how long will it be quiet? Put up thyself into thy scabbard rest, and be still."

We know that we go through storms in this life but we have Jesus to guide, lead, and protect us as He did during the sea storm, in which Jesus was sleeping and the disciples had awakened Him, telling him of the problem. It says in Mark 4:39, "And he arose, and rebuked the wind, and said unto the sea, 'Peace, be still.' And the wind ceased, and there was a great calm." For only Jesus can give us that type of peace.

We should be still to let God have His way in our everyday life, no matter how good or matter how bad it is, as long as we live it in His glory. It says in Hebrews 13:5, "Let your conversation be without covetousness; and be content with such things as ye have: for he hath said, I will never leave thee nor forsake thee." Now isn't that a good reason to be still in Him?

As we look to a man named Isaiah, who had seen God, who was willing to go where God wanted him to go and to do what God wanted him to do, it is written in Isaiah 42:14 as he exalts the Lord, "I have long time holden my peace;

I have been still, and refrained myself: now will I cry like a travailing woman; I will destroy and devour at once."

But here is a man who, as I have said before, has found favor in the eyes of God. That's David, who writes in many places in the Psalms about being still. To begin with in Psalms 4:4, he starts by saying, "Stand in awe, and sin not: commune with your own heart upon your bed, and be still."

In Psalms 8:2, David continues, saying, "Out of the mouth of babes and sucklings has thou ordained strength because of thine enemies, that thou mightiest still the enemy and the avenger." In Psalms 65:7 David speaks of God's power, saying, "Which stilleth the noise of the seas, the noise of their waves, and the tumult of the people." Surely only God, and God alone, can do all of these things.

In Psalms 76:8 David describes God's wrath, saying, "Thou didst cause judgment to be heard from Heaven; the earth feared, and was still." In Psalms 83:1, David cries out of Him with these words: "Keep not thou silence, O God: hold not thy peace, and be not still, O God."

In Psalms 107:29, David describes the mighty hand of God by telling us, "He maketh the storm a calm, so that the waves thereof are still."

But, in Psalms 46:10, David says more tellingly than in all the Psalms what we must do, and in this way we may obtain our instructions from the Lord and do greater works: "Be still, and know that I am God: I will be exalted among the heathen, I will be exhalted in the earth." Because of that, even the heathen and those in the earth will exalt Him, for if this doesn't tell you who has the final victory, I'm sure that His Word will show you when you remember to be still.

Done It Unto Me

(Matthew 25:40)

"And the King shall answer and say unto them, Verily I say unto you, inasmuch as ye have done it unto one of the least of these my brethren, ye have done it unto me." These things Jesus said to His disciples at the Mount of Olives and gave them this charge, not only to them, but to those who chose to carry-on in His name, telling what they are to do. When we do these things, we are to do them in a meek and humble spirit so that the Christ that lives in us shines for all the world to see.

Since we are to do anything and everything to His glory, it's only by His glory we can do these things for others, so that in these things, they may come to know who Jesus is. This will be showing those lost people, who are willing to see the true and risen Savior and who will take and lead them where they deserve to be, which is God's house.

We need to gather together in unity and love, not just for God, but for one another, because if we can't love one another, how can we love God?

It's recorded in Matthew 19:19 to, "Honour thy father and thy mother: and thou shalt love thy neighbour as thyself." But until we get past that roadblock, we cannot feel the full love that only God can give us.

It's only God and God alone who can place that perfect love. Not only that perfect love, but also that perfect peace that only Jesus can provide for us. For it is written in John 14:27 as Jesus speaks to Judas, not Iscariot, he says, "Peace I leave you, my peace I give unto you: not as the world giveth, give I unto you. Let not your heart be troubled, neither let it be afraid." Now what can't we do, according to what God wants us to do, in that type of peace?

When a man has everything, he cannot begin to cherish the little things, but when he has nothing then he can cherish everything that is given to him. Do not help one who has less than you with a heavy heart, because if it's done with no good intent and not for the glorification of God, He sees it and shall convict your heart for it.

So as you make your way in this world and you see someone in need, let the Holy Spirit guide your heart to do "unto one of the least of these brethren, ye have done it unto me."

What Is Your Vision?

(Proverbs 29:18)

Now that's an interesting question. Haven't
there been times when we have envisioned ourselves
in one way or another? But the main question is this:
is it to the glory of God? Because if God is not in the
big picture, then it's all for nothing!

But first, what is a vision? Well, it has several
definitions but I'll hit on a couple of them for you. One
has it being the faculty or sense of sight. Although we
are able to see with these mortal eyes, until we are
saved and washed in His blood, we are still blind.

In the Book of Acts, Paul was in front of
Agrippa speaking about his life and how he came to
know about Christ and in 26:19 summed it up by
saying, "Whereupon, O King Agrippa, I was not
disobedient unto the Heavenly vision."

A second definition of vision is the ability to
anticipate and make provision for future events;
foresight. But as Jeremiah wrote in Lamentations 2:9,
as he spoke about Jerusalem's misery, "Her gates are
sunk into the ground; he hath destroyed and broken

her bars: her king are her princes are among the Gentiles: the law is no more; her prophets also find no vision from the Lord." Also, as it's said in Micah 3:6 concerning false prophets, "Therefore night shall be unto you, that ye shall not have a vision; and it shall be dark unto you, that ye shall not divine; and the sun shall go down over the prophets, and the day shall be dark over them."

And Solomon, with all the wisdom that God had provided him with, knew the importance of having a vision, as he says in Proverbs 29:18: "Where there is no vision, the people perish: but he that keepeth the law, happy is he."

Also, in Habakkuk 2:1-3, it speaks of the importance of vision as it reads, "I will stand upon my watch, and set me upon the tower, and will watch to see what he will say unto me, and what I shall answer when I am reproved. And the Lord answered me and said, 'Write the vision, and make it plain upon tables, that he may run that readeth it. For the vision is yet for an appointed time, but at the end it shall speak, and not lie: though it tarry, wait for it; because it will surely come, it will not tarry.'"

The Bible speaks of people both young and old having vision. In 1 Samuel 3:1, the Lord comes upon Samuel as a child: "And the word of the Lord was precious in those days; there was no open vision." Even at an early age, Samuel was being instructed by the Lord to do His will.

In Matthew 17:9, Jesus, along with Peter, James, and John his brother were upon a high mountain where the vision of Moses and Elias appeared unto them. "And as they came down from the mountain, Jesus charged them, saying, 'Tell the vision to no man, until the Son of Man be risen again from the dead.'"

He had revealed to these disciples what was to happen, but they knew not. However it came to pass in Luke 24:23 that certain women made it known what happened to the body of Christ: "And when they found not his body, they came saying, that they had also seen a vision of angels, which said that he was alive."

If there be anyone who would know about a vision, it would be Paul, before he spoke to Agrippa on how Jesus appeared to him.

Also, in Acts 16:9 it relates, "and a vision appeared to Paul in the night; there stood a man of Macedonia, and prayed him, saying, 'come over into Macedonia, and help us.' "

Also in Acts 18:9 and 10 as well, while he was in Corinth preaching the Gospel to all the people and many were persuaded, another vision occurred: "Then spake the Lord to Paul in the night by a vision, 'Be not afraid, but speak, and hold not thy peace: for I am with thee, and no man shall set on thee to hurt thee: for I have much people in this city.' " So, brethren, as long as you walk with God and do those things in His glory, you will always remember what is your vision!

Perfect Peace

(Isaiah 26:3)

When I think of the goodness of the Lord, it baffles me to no absolute end because the things He has done are endless. When you think of all things He has done for you and the grace and mercy that He has been able to give to you, with a God like that, it's no small wonder that in Him you can have perfect peace.

I have spent eleven years in the U.S. Navy and I feel that these two stories can show you what God can and will do for you. I was not saved then and on my first ship, I was on watch at the time and the entire ship lost power. Now here's the setting: it's 2:00 a.m., no power, in the Black Sea, anywhere between twenty-five to fifty miles off the coast of Russia, and yes, there were Russian ships around. I don't know where, but they were there and not peaceful.

Part two goes as such: it was about two years later. We went south down to Grenada during the time that battle was happening. Let's see, it was early evening when a message came in for us to head south (because we had been on our way back stateside). Until everything started happening, we didn't know what was going on. All we did was patrol the northeastern part of the island, making sure nothing came in or out. But at this time, I had a small knowledge of God and was saved, so I had no fear, just an assurance of peace.

We know that there are things that Satan puts up in our face to scare and frighten us so that we don't act for God's glory. It says in 2 Timothy 1:7 when Paul writes to Timothy boldly, "For God hath not given us the spirit of fear; but of power, and of love, and of a sound mind." With such a testimony as that, he cannot help but give you perfect peace.

That is also one of God's names, which is Jehovah-Shalom: the lord is peace, so now you have a name that you can cry out to in those unsettling times and I know that He will give you that perfect peace. But only God can give us that perfect peace, for Isaiah says in 26:3 as the prophet is giving him praise, "Thou wilt keep him in perfect peace, whose mind is stayed on thee: because he trusteth in thee."

But you know that there's a difference between man's peace and God's peace. When man finds peace within himself, it's there, but something's missing. But when God puts His peace in you, there's nothing missing at all. So, brethren, remember this: man has an incomplete peace, but only God has complete and perfect peace and the only thing we strive for is to have perfect peace in Christ.

What Kind of Bread Do You Like?

(Matthew 4:4)

As a small child, like many others, I enjoyed many types of sandwiches using white bread. At breakfast, we had toast and at certain times, we had raisin toast for breakfast. During those days, I loved eating toast. I liked it so much that I made the toast my meal.

Now we have all kinds of bread; enriched bread, wheat bread, rye bread, raisin bread, potato bread, pita bread even way back when I used to call money bread (if you can think that far back!). But one bread is special. Why? Because if you look in John 6:48, we find Jesus speaks to the Jews, saying, "I am the Bread of Life." He goes further, saying in John 6:50 and 51, "This is the bread which cometh down from Heaven: If any man eat of this bread, he shall live for ever: and the bread that I will give is my flesh, which I will give for the life of the world." Now tell me, what kind of bread do you like?

We look now to the people who were brought out of Egypt by Moses and Aaron as they cried out in Exodus 16:3 and 4. "And the Children of Israel said unto them, 'Would to God we had died by the hand of the Lord in the land of Egypt, when we sat by the flesh pots, and when we did eat bread to the full; for ye have brought us forth into this wilderness, to kill this whole assembly with hunger.' Then said the Lord unto Moses, 'Behold I will rain bread from heaven for you; and the people shall go out and gather a certain rate every day, that I may prove them, whether they will walk in my law, or no." Now is this the kind of bread you want?

Further on in Exodus 23:25 as the laws were being given by Moses, they were informed that there was an angel before them to keep them and they were to obey him because God's name was in him, it says "And ye shall serve the Lord your God, and he shall bless thy bread, and thy water; and I will take sickness away from the midst of thee."

When the Levites had known what God did through his servant Moses, it says in Nehemiah 9:15: "And gavest them bread from heaven for them out of rock for their thirst, and promisedst them that they should go in and possess the land which thou hadst sworn to give them."

In Deuteronomy 8:3 where Moses gave out God's law, he reminded them how God had fed them in the wilderness: "And he humbled thee, and suffered thee to hunger, and fed thee with manna, which thou knewest not, neither did thy fathers know; that he might make thee know that man doth not live by bread only, but by every word that proceedeth out of the mouth of the Lord doth man live."

Jesus, after being in the wilderness for forty days, was being tempted by Satan, as it's written in Matthew 4:3 and 4: "And when the tempter came to him, he said, 'if thou be the Son of God, command that these stones be made bread.' But he answered and said, 'It is written, man shall not live by bread alone, but by every word that proceedeth out of the mouth of God.'" Now that's real bread to feed from.

Now the following should be known to each and every believer. When the disciples and Christ were gathered together in the Upper Room for the Lord's Supper, Jesus, after letting all know who would betray him, did this in Matthew 26:26: "And as they were eating, Jesus took bread, and blessed it, and brake it, and gave it to the disciples, and said, 'Take, eat; this is my body.' "

Even in our prayers, God shows how important bread is. In Luke 11:3 it says, "Give us day by day our daily bread." So even further on in Luke 14:15, after Christ had taught the disciples to care for the poor, "And when one of them that sat at meat with him heard these things, he said unto him, 'Blessed is he that shall eat bread in the kingdom of God.' "

Now Sennacherib, King of Assyria, as he turned his back on Hezekiah, who during that time was King of Judah, had men hearken unto him as he besieged Jerusalem. His envoys appeal to the Jews in 2 Kings 18:32: "Until I come and take you away to a land like your own land, a land of corn and wine, a land of bread and vineyard, a land of olive oil and of honey, that ye may live, and not die; and hearken not unto Hezekiah, when he persuadeth you, saying, 'The Lord will deliver us.' "

As we now see bread's importance in Psalms, where in 132:15, David tells us of God's faithfulness of his promises: "I will abundantly bless her provision: I will, satisfy her poor with bread." In Proverbs 31:27, in which Solomon speaks of the praises of a good wife, he says, "She looketh well to the ways of her household, and eateth not the bread of idleness."

As Amos spoke to an Israel that was being incapable of being reformed or chastened, he says in Amos 4:6, "And I also have given you cleanness of teeth in all your cities, and want of bread in all your places: yet have ye not returned unto me, saith the Lord."

In Mark, Jesus and His disciples had arrived in Nazareth, His home, and saw these same people who should have known Him best, turned away due to their unbelief. In Mark 6:8, the twelve were sent two by two and were given power over unclean spirits: "And commanded them that they should take nothing

69

for their journey, save a staff only; no scrip, no bread, no money in their purse." Further on in Mark 7:27 to 29, a woman who came to Christ, out of faith to ask that He cast out the devil from her daughter, "but Jesus said unto her 'Let the children first be filled: for it is not meet to take the children's bread, and to cast it unto the dogs.' And she answered and said unto him, 'Yes, Lord: yet the dogs under the table eat of the children's crumbs.' And he said unto her, 'For this saying go thy way; the devil is gone out of thy daughter.' " This saying, "go thy way; the devil is gone out of thy daughter," follows mention of the bread that is faith. It is knowing what God can and will do and that all we have to do is believe and take it to Him.

Now we return to John, in which after the people were fed by five loaves and two fish and were filled, they sought Jesus and found Him and asked Him for signs that they could see and believe how God worked through Jesus. And John 6:32 to 35, this exchange goes: "Then Jesus said unto them, 'Verily , verily, I say unto you, Moses gave you not that bread from Heaven; but my Father giveth you the true bread from Heaven. For the Bread of God is he which cometh down from Heaven, and giveth life unto the world.' Then said they unto him, 'Lord, evermore give us this bread.' And Jesus said unto them, 'I am the bread of life: he that cometh to me shall never hunger, and he that believeth on me shall never thirst.' " Now this is the kind of bread that I like, don't you?

Finish What You Started

(Revelation 22:13)

"I am Alpha and Omega, the beginning and the end,
the first and the last."

This is what Jesus said to John as he showed
him paradise because that is what Heaven is for
those who accept Jesus Christ freely and fully as Lord
and Savior of their lives. Because only God, and God
all by Himself, can do it; He started it and whatever
He starts, He sees it to its total completeness.

It says that He started it all in the very first
verse in Genesis 1:1: "In the beginning God created
the heaven and the earth." He began creation of the
earth, so you know he sees its destruction and
reconstruction. But so many times in our everyday
lives, we start on one thing, but never see it to its
completion.

For as Paul stated in Philippians 1:6, as he
wrote to the Church of Philippi, "Being confident of
this very thing, that he which hath begun a good work
in you will perform it until the day of Jesus Christ."

And he speaks as well in 2 Corinthians 8:6 telling them to note how God graced the churches of Macedonia and informing them that "Insomuch that we desired Titus, that as he had begun, so he would also finish in you the same grace also." In this, Paul is allowing Titus to finish what he started.

Because Christ sees everything from beginning to end, shouldn't we? Even now, Christ is working on us, but we know that once it's done, it's perfect! God has a way of repeating Himself in His Word, but in this case, it is not twice, but perhaps three times. He is this "I Am," which is not only the last one in the Bible, but perhaps the most powerful one of all.

He says in Revelation 1:8, when He spoke to John, saying, "I am Alpha and Omega, the beginning and the ending, saith the Lord, which is, and which was, and which is to come, the Almighty." Further down in verse 11, Jesus says and instructs John, "Saying, 'I am Alpha and Omega, the first and the last: and, what thou seest, write in a book, and send it unto the seven churches which are in Asia;

unto Ephesus, and unto Smyrna, and unto Pergamos, and unto Thyatira, and unto Sardis, and unto Philadelphia, and unto Laodicea.' "

As we continue in Revelation, where John saw a new Heaven and a new earth and a new Jerusalem, with all the joy and glory, he hears a voice instructing him to write in Revelation 21:6: "And he said unto me, 'It is done. I'm Alpha and Omega, the beginning and the end. I will give unto him that is athirst of the fountain of the water of life freely,' " which should let you know by this time that he began everything and when it's all said and done, he ends everything.

In John, when the Jews, hearing that Jesus healed a man on the Sabbath, were angry and wanted to kill Him and more so when He told them that God was His Father. In John 5:36, He spoke unto them, "But I have greater witness than that of John: for the works which the Father hath given me to finish, the same works that I do, bear witness of me, that the Father hath sent me.

Later, as Jesus knew that the time to rejoin God in Heaven was at hand, He prays in John chapter 17, at one point in particular, in verse 4, saying, "I have glorified thee on the earth: I have finished the work which thou gavest me to do." All that was left for Jesus to do, was to take our sins on His shoulders because no one else can and will do it.

As he hung from the cross for the completion of this earthly mission, bearing pain and sorrow that came from bearing the sins of the world, John 19:30 tells us what happened, "When Jesus therefore has received the vinegar, he said, 'It is finished' and he bowed his head, and gave up the ghost."

Paul was a devoted man to Christ after the day he met Him on his way to Damascus, which forever changed his life. He had started his work, but now as we see in 2 Timothy 4:7 as his end is near, he reminds Timothy to continue the fight, but for Paul himself says, "I have fought a good fight, I have finished my course, I have kept the faith." Remember these words, so you can be able to finish what you started!

Ten More Things to Remember

1. To build a relationship with Christ, it must be built upon this rock!
2. Satan will always try to trip you up, so watch your step!
3. Always look to God for wisdom and understanding!
4. Are you pressed to do the things that Christ wants you to do?
5. To know God's true purpose, we have to be still!
6. When you do anything in God's glory, remember how to have "done it unto me!"
7. Stay with Jesus, and He will show you what is your vision.
8. Trusting in Christ, gives you perfect peace!
9. What kind of bread do you like? It should be bread from Heaven!
10. Finish what you started and He will bless you to no end!

Selah!

CPSIA information can be obtained
at www.ICGtesting.com
Printed in the USA
LVHW031748130121
676401LV00007B/834